## 21st Century Skills Library

REAL WORLD MATH: PERSONAL FINANCE

# INVESTING:
## MAKING YOUR MONEY WORK FOR YOU

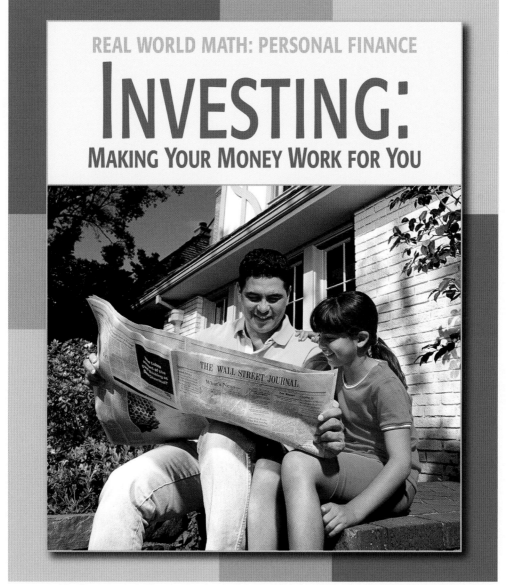

*Cecilia Minden*

**Cherry Lake Publishing**
**Ann Arbor, Michigan**

Published in the United States of America by Cherry Lake Publishing
Ann Arbor, MI
www.cherrylakepublishing.com

Math Education Adviser: Timothy J. Whiteford, PhD, Associate Professor of Education, St. Michael's College, Colchester, Vermont

Finance Adviser: Ryan Spaude, CFP®, Kitchenmaster Financial Services, LLC, North Mankato, Minnesota

Photo Credits: Cover and page 1, © Brian Leng/Corbis; page 15, © James Leynse/Corbis; page 17, © Orjan F. Ellingvag/Dagens Naringsliv/Corbis

Library of Congress Cataloging-in-Publication Data
Minden, Cecilia.
 Investing : making your money work for you / by Cecilia Minden.
    p. cm. — (Real world math. Personal finance)
  ISBN-13: 978-1-60279-003-2
  ISBN-10: 1-60279-003-5
 1. Investments—Juvenile literature. 2. Saving and investment—Juvenile literature. 3. Stocks—Juvenile literature. 4. Children—Finance, Personal—Juvenile literature. I. Title. II. Series.
  HG4521.M47 2008
  332.6—dc22                                    2007005917

Cherry Lake Publishing would like to acknowledge the work of
The Partnership for 21st Century Skills.
Please visit www.21stcenturyskills.org for more information.

# TABLE OF CONTENTS

## CHAPTER ONE

# WHAT IS INVESTING?

*Money doesn't grow on trees, but if you make smart investments it will seem like your money is growing.*

Have you heard the expression, "Money doesn't grow on trees"? Maybe

you heard it the last time you asked your parents for money! Well, money

may not grow on trees, but you *can* get your money to grow. You do it by investing. Investing means you purchase something of value, with the expectation that it will make you more money.

To understand investing, you have to understand some terms. Here are a few terms to get you started. You will learn more terms as you read about different ways to invest.

Inflation is one reason to invest money. Inflation means that prices go up. Years ago, farmers brought vegetables to town markets in horse-drawn wagons. Back then, vegetables cost pennies. Most vegetables today are still sold in markets in towns. Farmers are still paid, but so are the people who own the markets. Shipping, storage, and other expenses also raise the cost. Vegetables are still vegetables, but today they cost hundreds of times more to buy.

The cost of living is the money you need to cover your needs. Everyone needs a home, food, and clothing. When inflation goes up, so does the cost of living.

Financial goals are plans for the future. You need to plan so that when inflation goes up, you have enough money to pay for your living expenses. There are two types of financial goals: short-term goals and long-term goals. Short-term goals pay for things that you will buy in a few weeks or months. Short-term goals might include paying for a trip, a bike, or a computer. Long-term goals pay for things far into the future. These might include college tuition or starting a business.

There are several different ways you can invest your money. Let's see which one works best for you!

## CHAPTER TWO

# SAVINGS OPTIONS

The best way to have money for the future is to make money today and save it. Three places you can invest the money you save are in savings accounts, certificates of deposit, and government bonds.

*You are loaning money to the U.S. government when you buy a savings bond.*

The most basic form of investment is a savings account. By putting your money in a savings account, your money can earn you more money. Banks will pay you money, called interest, to keep your money with them. Savings accounts allow you to take money out whenever you need it. Because of this, savings accounts are good places to keep money for short-term goals. Banks offer only low interest rates on savings accounts.

Certificates of deposit (CDs) are another way to save. When you buy a CD, you are putting your money in a special kind of bank account. CDs are sold in fixed amounts such as $500 or $1,000. By purchasing a CD, you agree to leave money in that account for a certain

length of time, such as one year. When the time is up, you can withdraw

your money plus the interest you earned. If you take your money out of

*A nearby automated teller machine (ATM) can make it*
*convenient to deposit money in your savings account.*

the CD account early, you are charged a penalty. Usually, the penalty is

that you lose a lot of the interest money you earned. Banks offer higher

rates on CDs than on savings accounts because the bank knows it will have

your money for a certain length of time.

## REAL WORLD MATH CHALLENGE

Catherine purchases three one-year CDs for $2,000 each. The CDs earn 5.2 percent interest per year. **How much interest will Catherine earn on the CDs in one year?**

*(Turn to page 29 for the answer)*

Government bonds are another place you can invest your money. If

a city government needs to raise money for an expensive project, such as

building a hospital, it might sell bonds. When you purchase government

bonds, you are loaning the government money. The government agrees to

pay you a certain interest rate, called a dividend yield. But you cannot get

*Sometimes bonds are sold to raise money for an
expensive government construction project.*

your money out for a specific length of time, often 10 years. Bonds are a

safe investment, but the amount of money you make is usually low.

Savings accounts, CDs, and government  bonds are all safe ways to

invest your money. There is almost no chance you will lose money with

these investments. Though the interest is usually not very high, you'll

*Banks send out statements each month that show how much interest your money has earned. They also list all the deposits and withdrawals that you have made.*

know exactly how much you will earn. Other types of investments offer

the chance to earn more interest. Which is the right choice for you? Let's

find out!

## CHAPTER THREE

# Do the Math:
# Making More at the Bank

*A good investment plan can help you save money
for a new car or other expensive item.*

Samantha has saved $3,000 from her part-time job and money her

grandparents gave her for her birthday. She wants to buy a car in the next year.

She's hoping to earn as much interest as possible on her savings. Samantha

**21st Century Content**

In the 1930s, many banks went out of business. Thousands of people lost all of their money. The Federal Deposit Insurance Corporation (FDIC) was formed to keep this from happening again. The FDIC insures bank accounts for amounts worth up to $100,000. With the FDIC, even if the bank is robbed or burns down or goes out of business, you will always get your money back.

can't buy savings bonds because she's going to need the money in less than a year. She doesn't want to put the money into CDs because she doesn't know exactly when she'll find the car of her dreams and need to withdraw her money. And her savings account is only getting 1 percent interest. What should she do with her savings?

A friend recommends she put it into a money market account. Money market accounts usually earn much higher interest than regular savings accounts. You handle a money market account much like a savings account, but it comes with more restrictions. Money market accounts usually require a minimum balance. This means you must keep a

*The Federal Deposit Insurance Company insures the money in your bank account up to $100,000. It is headquartered in Washington, DC.*

certain amount of money in the account. If you go below that balance,

you will have to pay a penalty. And with many money market accounts,

you may be limited to a certain number of withdrawals a month.

## REAL WORLD MATH CHALLENGE

Frank worked all summer mowing lawns. By the end of the summer, he had saved $1,400. He wants to invest his money. Frank wants to keep all his money at one bank. **Which investment will earn him the most interest**?

**Savings Account:** Red Bank is offering 3.6 percent annual interest on a minimum deposit of $1,000.

**Certificate of Deposit:** Blue Bank is offering 5.1 percent interest on a 1-year $1,000 CD.

**Money Market Account:** White Bank is offering 4 percent annual interest on a money market account. Frank can make three withdrawals on his account without penalty if he keeps a balance of $1,000.

*(Turn to page 29 for the answer)*

Like savings accounts, money market accounts are a safe place to invest your money. Though they usually pay much more interest than savings accounts, the interest rate is still not high. Would you like your money to earn you even more money? You may have to take a chance of losing some money. Is it worth the risk? Let's find out!

## CHAPTER FOUR

# DO THE MATH: STOCKS

*Stock traders work on the floor of the New York Stock Exchange (NYSE).*

Money market accounts, CDs, and government bonds are simple

and safe ways to invest your money. A different type of investment is

purchasing stock in a company. When you buy stock in a company, you

are buying part of the company. You share in the company's profits—and

its losses. Here's how it works.

When you buy stock (or shares) in a company, you become part owner of the company. You will make or lose money, depending on the company's success.

There are two ways you can make money with stock. When companies make profits, you may receive payments called dividends. The more stock you own, the more money you will get from dividends. A second way people make money with stocks is by selling stock for more money than they paid for it.

How much people are willing to pay for a company's stock changes over time. If the company is making a lot of profit or has a bright future, people will be willing to pay more for the stock. On the flip side, if a company's profits are dropping or it has legal problems, people will not pay as much for its stock. If you sell the stock for less than you paid for it, you lose money.

Many people hold on to the same stock for decades. They aren't buying and selling the stock, so they aren't making money that they can spend right away. But over the years, if the company does well, the value of their stock rises. Perhaps when they retire, they sell the stock. By then, it might be worth 50 times what they paid for it. The profit helps pay their living expenses.

Investing in stocks has many advantages. You can be a part of something you believe in or like. If you support environmental issues, you might invest in a company that researches new fuels. Maybe you like video games, and there's a company that has a new

Many people use a stockbroker to help them purchase stocks. A stockbroker is someone who buys and sells stocks for others.

Even though you take advantage of a stockbroker's expert knowledge, it is important to take responsibility for your investments. Try to learn as much as you can about the companies your money is invested in. Make sure that they are companies that reflect your values.

game you think will be a big hit. You can buy stock in that company. The

best part is that you are using your money to make more money for your

financial goals.

There are also disadvantages to investing in stocks. The biggest

one, of course, is that you can lose part or all of your money. It's a risk

## REAL WORLD MATH CHALLENGE

In January, Elena purchased 25 shares of TECHEEGAMES for $32 a share. At the end of six months, the stock went up to $46 a share. **How much was Elena's investment in the stock worth in January? How much was her investment worth in June? How much money did Elena gain?**

Elena took $350 out of her savings account to purchase more shares of TECHEEGAMES. **How many more shares did Elena buy with her savings?** (Hint: you can only buy whole shares.) **How many total shares did she then have?**

In August, TECHEEGAMES stock went down to $34 a share. **How much was her investment in the stock worth then? How much more money would she have had if she had sold all her stock in June?**

*(Turn to page 29 for the answers)*

*Wall Street is the heart of New York City's financial district.*

because the Federal Deposit Insurance Corporation

(FDIC) does not insure money invested in stocks.

You are investing without any insurance. Another

disadvantage is that if your money is tied up in stocks, you can't use it for other things.

Investing in the stock market takes research and patience. Read articles and listen to financial reports relating to that stock. Do not try to "time the market." When you time the market, you are hoping to make a big profit by buying when stocks are low and selling when stocks are high. It sounds easy, but not many people can do it successfully. Taking a risk is part of investing. You may lose money. The important thing is to do your homework. Knowing everything you can about a company before investing in it will help limit your losses and increase your profits.

## CHAPTER FIVE

# KEEPING YOUR BALANCE

*A part-time job in a store or office can provide you
with the money you need to begin investing.*

Miguel is 16 years old. He just started working at the bookstore two

afternoons a week and all day on Saturday. It is exciting getting a paycheck

every week, and he wants to make sure he puts his money to good use.

Miguel wants to buy a new computer. That's a short-term goal. He is also saving money for college. That's a long-term goal. He is even hoping to

put a little money away so that eventually he will be able to buy a house.

Miguel has a savings account, and his uncle gave him 20 shares of Wintech

stock when he was born. But now that he has a steady income, he wants to

start investing more.

*There are many computer programs that can help
you keep track of your investments.*

Miguel decides to sit down with his parents to talk about his portfolio. A portfolio is a collection of savings and investments. Miguel's parents discuss three ways he can build his portfolio:

- Invest a steady amount each month to cover short-term and long-term goals.

- Put extra money into long-term investments.

- Diversify his portfolio by placing money in different types of investments.

Like Miguel, if you want to reach your short-term and long-term goals, you need to make investing a priority. Decide what part of each paycheck will be set aside for investments. Use part of it for your short-term goals. These are things you want to buy or do within a few weeks or months. Place that money where it will earn interest but can be withdrawn without

*A good investment strategy can help you save money for college.*

penalty. Use the rest of your investment money for long-term goals.

College or retirement seems far away to you now. That day will come,

however, and a long-term investment will help cover your expenses.

Putting money into investments is a little like having a private money

machine. Others are paying you to let them use your money. All you have to do is have patience and wait. Over the long term, that money is going to work for you and make a profit.

Diversifying your portfolio helps keep your investments safe. There are many places you can invest your money, including stocks, bonds, and CDs. When your money is spread out over several investments, you lower the risk of losing all your money. Putting money in different investments also helps you learn more about how different companies work and allows you to support different causes that are important to you.

Before you start investing, you need to do research. Begin by picking a couple of stocks in the

*You can find information about stocks and other investments in the business section of your newspaper.*

newspaper. Track them for a month. Keep a chart of the ups and downs of the stock price. Also pay attention to interest paid at local banks. Talk to people who are already investing. Check out the books and Web sites listed at the end of this book. Record your information and use it to help you decide on the best investments for you.

Always remember that the less you spend, the more you save. The more you save, the more you have to invest. And the more you invest, the more your money can earn money for you!

# REAL WORLD MATH CHALLENGE ANSWERS

## Chapter Two

**Page 10**

Catherine will earn $312 in interest in one year.

$2,000 × 3 = $6,000

5.2% of $6,000 = 0.052 × $6,000 = $312

## Chapter Three

**Page 16**

Frank would earn $50.40 with the savings account, $51.00 with the CD, and $56.00 with the money market account. If he is using only one bank, Frank would make the most interest by investing in the money market account.

3.6% of $1,400 = 0.036 × $1,400 = $50.40

5.1% of $1,000 = 0.051 × $1,000 = $51.00

4% of $1,400 = 0.04 × $1,400 = $56.00

Frank would make the most money if he split his money between the CD and the savings account. He could earn $51.00 in interest on a $1,000 CD. If he put the remaining $400 in a savings account, it would earn $14.40 in interest. He would make a total of $65.40 in interest.

5.1% of $1,000 = 0.051 × $1,000 = $51.00

3.6% of $400 = 0.036 × $400 = $14.40

$51.00 + $14.40 = $65.40

## Chapter Four

**Page 20**

In January, Elena's investment in the stock was worth $800. By June, the value of her investment in the stock had risen to $1,150. The value of Elena's investment had increased $350.

25 × $32.00 = $800

25 × $46.00 = $1,150

$1,150 − $800 = $350

Elena bought 7 more shares in June. She had 32 total shares.

$350 ÷ $46.00 = 7.6

25 + 7 = 32

In August, the value of Elena's investment in the stock dropped to $1,088. If she had sold it all in June, she would have made $1,150, or $62.00 more than in August.

32 × $34.00 = $1,088

$1,150 − $1,088 = $62.00

# Glossary

balance (BA-lunts) the amount of money in a bank account

diversify (duh-VUR-suh-fie) to place money in several different types of investments

dividends (DIH-vuh-dendz) money paid to shareholders out of a company's profits

inflation (in-FLAY-shun) the rising cost of goods and services

interest (IN-trest) the amount earned on money kept in a bank

penalty (PEH-nul-tee) a fee charged when an agreement is broken

portfolio (port-FOE-lee-oh) a group of investments owned by one person

stock (STOK) a certificate that proves part ownership in a company

# FOR MORE INFORMATION

## Books

Bateman, Katherine Roberta. *The Young Investor: Projects and Activities for Making Your Money Grow.* Chicago: Chicago Review Press, 2001.

Condon, Daniel. *Playing the Market: Stocks and Bonds.* Chicago: Heinemann Library, 2003.

Karlitz, Gail. *Growing Money: A Complete Investing Guide for Kids.* New York: Price Stern Sloan, 2001.

## Web Sites

### 401Kidz: Cool Investments
*www.401kidz.com/investment/typesofinv.asp*
Information on different kinds of savings accounts for kids

### Moneyopolis: Where Money Sense Rules!
*www.moneyopolis.org/new/home.asp*
Money games and information

### Young Investor
*www.younginvestor.com/*
Information on investing and puzzles and other games

# INDEX

# ABOUT THE AUTHOR

Cecilia Minden, PhD, is a literacy consultant and the author of many books for children. She is the former director of the Language and Literacy Program at Harvard Graduate School of Education in Cambridge, Massachusetts. She would like to thank fifth-grade math teacher Beth Rottinghaus for her help with the Real World Math Challenges. Cecilia lives with her family in North Carolina.